**FESTIVALS AND FAITHS**

# CHRISTMAS

## CATHERINE CHAMBERS

Evans

First published in this edition in 2010 by
Evans Brothers Limited
2A Portman Mansions
Chiltern Street
London W1U 6NR

British Library Cataloguing in Publication Data
Chambers, Catherine, 1954-
    Christmas. -- (Festivals and faiths)
    1. Christmas--Juvenile literature.
    I. Title II. Series
    394.2'663-dc22

ISBN 978 0 237 54119 4

Printed in China

# ACKNOWLEDGEMENTS

**Editor:**  Su Swallow
**Design:**  Neil Sayer
**Production:**  Jenny Mulvanny

For permission to reproduce copyright material, the
author and publishers gratefully acknowledge the fol-
lowing:

**Cover:** (top) Collections/Geoff Howard, (bottom
and back) Circa Photo Library/John Fryer
**Contents pages:** Zefa **page 6** Circa Photo
Library/John Fryer **page 7** (top) Zefa, (bottom)
Jennie Woodcock, Reflections Photo Library **page 8**
Garo Nalbandian/Roberr Harding Picture Library
**page 9** Andrew Ward/Life File **page 10** (top) Zefa,
(bottom) Chris Bland/Eye Ubiquitous **page 11** Hans
Reinhard/Bruce Coleman **page 12** (top) trip/V
Kolpakov, (bottom) Collections /Geoff Howard **page
13** Circa Photo Library **page 14** (top) Romilly
Lockyer/Image Bank, (bottom) James Davis Travel
Photography **page 15** Ellen Rooney/Robert Harding
Picture Library **page 16** Robert Harding Picture
Library **page 17** (top) Zefa, (bottom) Trip/H Rogers
**page 18** Private Collection/Bridgeman Art Library
**page 19** (top left) Trip/H Rogers, (top right) David
Hurn/Magunm, (bottom) H. Gruyaert/Magnum
**page 20** (top) Zefa, Jennie
Woodcock/Reflections Photo Library **page 21** Mayer-
Magunm **page 22** (top) Trip/A Tjagny-Rjadno (bot-
tom) Food Features **page 23** Robert Harding Picture
Library **page 24** Gerard Champlong/Image Bank
**page 25** (left) Blair Seitz/Photo Researchers, Inc.
(right) Alan Becker/Image Bank **page 26** Hermitage,
St. Petersburg/Bridgeman Art Library **page 27** (left)
Nigel Sitwell/Life File, (right) Micha bar
Am/Magnum **page 28/29** Alan Towse Photography

# Contents

# The meaning of Christmas

CHRISTMAS! It means so many things. For Christians all over the world it celebrates the birth of Christ. For others it is a chance to show caring and giving. Long ago, winter parties brightened the dark days and honoured the sun.

## CHRISTMAS BEGINNINGS

The dazzling colour and light of Christmas celebrates the birth of just one baby, Jesus Christ. He was born over 2,000 years ago in Palestine. But Jesus Christ was no ordinary baby. When He grew up, His life and teachings were so powerful that people wanted to follow them. These people were called Christians.

A manger scene shows Jesus Christ and Mary, His mother. Shepherds and the three Kings kneel down to worship Him.

Angels and a Christmas tree light up New York's Rockefeller Centre.

It's fun decorating the Christmas tree with shiny balls.

## IN THE BLEAK MIDWINTER

The Christian Church only decided to celebrate Chrismas about 350 years after Jesus was born. No one really knows exactly when His birthday was. But Christmas has always been celebrated in either December or January. This fitted in well with ancient winter festivals in North Africa and Europe. Ceremonies were held to make the sun shine again in the spring and to bring good harvests.

When is the special day? Before Jesus was born, some people celebrated the birth of a different holy baby. It was the Persian god, Mithra - born on the 25th December. This is the day when most Christians now celebrate Christmas. So perhaps the two festivals were joined together. Other Christians in parts of Europe celebrate on the 6th January. Some Armenians wait until the 17th!

Caring and giving were a normal part of many winter festivals. And there's someone who fits in well with this tradition. Yes, it's Santa Claus!

7

# The Christmas story

THE HOLY BIBLE is one of many ancient books about God. It was written in this book that one day, a special baby would be born, bringing joy and light to the world. His name was Jesus.

This is the town of Bethlehem, where Jesus Christ was born. You can see the hills where the shepherds watched over their sheep.

After Jesus was born, Mary and Joseph had to flee from King Herod. Mary and Jesus were carried on a donkey.

## THE NEWBORN KING

About 2000 years ago, a carpenter called Joseph and his wife, Mary, had been chosen by God to have this special baby. They both knew this was true, because angels had told them so.

At that time, there was a mean ruler in Palestine called King Herod. Just before Jesus was born, Herod ordered all the people in the land to go back to the place where they had been born. There, they would all be counted. So Joseph took Mary with him on a long journey to his birthplace - a small town called Bethlehem. Mary felt really tired when they got there - she knew that the baby would soon be born. Joseph tried to find them a place to stay but all the small hotels were full. Hundreds of people had come to be counted.

Joseph was getting desperate - there was no room anywhere. Finally he found a kind hotel keeper who showed them to the only room he had - a stable, carved out of rock. Inside, there was an ox and an ass, lots of straw and not much else. It was here in this poor stable that Jesus Christ was born.

## SHEPHERDS AND KINGS COME TO WORSHIP

That night on the chilly hills around Bethlehem, shepherds were looking after their sheep. It seemed like every other night until a flash of light blinded them. When their eyes had cleared the shepherds saw an angel. He told them to leave their sheep and follow the bright star that shone over the stable. There, they would find the Son of God. When the shepherds got there, they knelt down at the feet of Jesus.

Later, three kings arrived from far-off lands. Their advisors had told them that a great king had been born. The three kings offered rich gifts to the baby.

# A glow in winter

The EARLY LEADERS of the Christian Church in Rome wanted people to accept new Christian customs. But they let people keep their old festivals, too. It made the people feel much happier about being Christians.

Winter festivals were held in cold, snowy villages – like this one in Norway.

## THE OLD AND THE NEW

The Romans helped to spread Christianity as they marched through their huge empire - from the Middle East as far west as Ireland. But they brought other religious customs, too. And it was quite alright to take part in a mixture of customs.

Romans celebrated the sun in winter. They often carved pictures of the sun. People have made sun carvings ever since – like this one on a sundial.

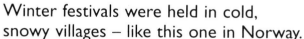

The Romans wanted a warm sun and rich harvests in the year to come. So during winter, they held a seven-day feast to honour Saturn. He was the god of farming. He kept everyone well fed! At the feast, candles were lit. People gave each other presents and little dolls made of clay or pastry. Green-leaved branches were plucked for decoration. That's like some of our Christmas customs today.

Wherever the Romans went, they discovered that other people had winter festivals, too. In Britain and northern France, they found that the Celts held a winter celebration. We get the tradition of kissing under the mistletoe from the Celts. What a mixture our Christmas traditions are!

Mistletoe invites kisses at Christmas. It usually grows on apple trees!

# Carols, chimes and pantomimes

**F**ROM CAROL-SINGERS to bell-ringers, music has been an important part of Christmas for hundreds of years. Plays and pantomimes are important too.

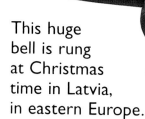

This huge bell is rung at Christmas time in Latvia, in eastern Europe.

## SINGING IN A CIRCLE

Handbells and church bells are rung at Christmas to mark the birth of Christ. But what about the Christmas carol?

Long ago in many parts of Europe, carols were just songs that were sung by people standing in a circle. They were sung at all kinds of festival.

A few hundred years after the birth of Christ, special carols were written for Christmas. They were not like the dull church hymns of

Choir boys singing Christmas carols in London's Westminster Abbey

the time, written in Latin - a language that few people understood. Carols were songs for ordinary folk, written in their own language. The songs were simple and joyful, and people could sing them anywhere, not just in church.

About 500 years ago, some very strict Christians, the Puritans, stopped people from singing carols. Carols sounded too happy! For 200 years, there were only a few parts of Europe where people dared to sing

them. But the tradition survived, especially in parts of France, Germany and Britain. Now they are written and sung by Christians in all corners of the world.

## MIMING AND RHYMING

There's plenty of entertainment at Christmas time. Many people perform nativity plays about Mary and Joseph's journey to Bethlehem. Long ago, all over the Christian world, people performed miracle plays, which were about the Christmas story. But they also staged folk tales. The actors, known as mummers, wore strange costumes and mimed and danced the stories. In England about 200 years ago, the plays were spoken in rhyme. Later, they turned into what is known today as pantomime!

A nativity play is acted out by school children. In the back row you can see shepherds, the angel and the three kings.

# The holly and the ivy

CRACKERS, TREES AND PAPER CHAINS are all well-known Christmas decorations. Long ago, houses were draped with holly, ivy and mistletoe.

## MISTLETOE MYSTERY

In ancient midwinter festivals, people draped holly, ivy and evergreen boughs around their houses - and over each other! They believed it would bring back the sun. But mistletoe was probably the most special decoration of all. Its clusters of pale green berries, like little lights, would surely make the sun shine? But for Christians, mistletoe was too closely connected with these old religions. You will still see holly and ivy in churches, but rarely the mistletoe.

## AND A BABY, LYING IN A MANGER

If you open a church door at Christmas time, you are almost sure to see a stable scene, glowing in the dim light. With models of Joseph, Mary, the baby lying in a manger and the shepherds, it reminds people of what Christmas means to them. These models became part of the Christian Christmas in 1224, when

Holly and ivy decorate this manger scene.

A Christmas tree in Prague in the Czech Republic, covered in tiny white lights. Some people put a star at the top of the tree. Others put a doll or an angel there instead.

Saint Francis of Assisi made the first nativity scene. He loved animals. So you will find an ox and an ass in the stable as well.

## OH, CHRISTMAS TREE! OH, CHRISTMAS TREE!

The biggest decoration of all is probably the Christmas tree. This custom started in the German Black Forest. Here, the dark evergreen trees grow so thickly over the hillsides that it makes them look black. The tradition spread through the rest of Germany and Europe about 200 years ago. German settlers took it to America, too. Today, you can see Christmas trees in all corners of the world, though many are made of plastic! But what do these trees strung with lights mean? Some say that the dark green leaves are the night sky, and the tinsel and lights are the stars.

15

# Calendars and crowns

CHRISTMAS IS COMING! In churches all over the world, Christians prepare for the religious celebration. Shops are full of people buying presents!

## READY, STEADY, GO!

You can probably find Christmas presents in the shops as early as October. Lights and decorations glow in the streets from November. But the Christian Church does not start to get ready for Christmas until the fourth Sunday before the 25th December - the big day for most people.

This time of preparation is called Advent. It means 'the coming'. It began over 1500 years ago. It is celebrated on the last four Sundays before Christmas.

The Church wanted Christians to see the birth of Christ as a light shining in a world of darkness.

So on the first Sunday of Advent, darkened churches held very sad,

Christmas shoppers search the shop windows for presents to buy.

16

This church in Jerusalem is dark during Advent.

solemn services. They got a little bit brighter and more cheerful on the next Sunday, and so on. On Christmas Day, joy and light shone in every church!

## On the night before Christmas

Carol-singing and party games, mistletoe-kissing and midnight mass. This is how people in many parts of the world celebrate Christmas Eve. Each country has its own traditions as well as the ones that most of us share. In southern Portugal, plates are piled high with crisp, sticky pastries. Families gather and presents are handed out. For here, Christmas Eve is the main celebration. In Denmark, people fast, eating only rice. Italians serve up fish dishes. There are so many different traditions!

At Advent nowadays, children in many parts of the world open the first door of an Advent calendar on 1st December - and the last door on Christmas Eve.

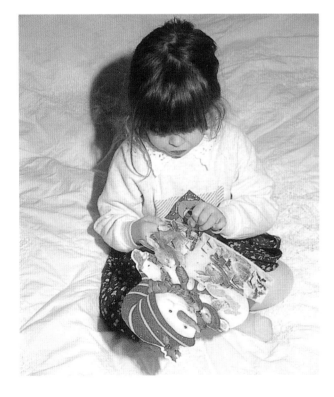

On 1st December a child opens the first of 24 doors of an Advent calendar. The last is opened on Christmas Eve.

# Santa Claus is coming!

Father Christmas is weighed down with presents on this Victorian Christmas card.

WHO IS SANTA CLAUS - or Father Christmas? How does he fit into the Christmas festival? The mystery began hundreds of years ago and in many different places!

## GIVING AND CARING

Some people say that the first Santa Claus came from Carthage in North Africa. He was a greedy god who gobbled up all his presents, which were. . . children! I don't think I'd leave out a plate of mince pies for him!

Others say that he was the Roman god, Saturn, or even the Viking god, Odin. Perhaps he started off as one of the green fairy gods with horns on their heads from many parts of Europe. All these gods were kind and generous at winter time, when people held festivals to honour them.

The Christmas story fits in well with these ancient traditions of giving. The shepherds and later, the three kings, offered gifts to Jesus.

A picture of St Nicholas in a Greek Orthodox Church.

Children in Switzerland join a St Nicholas parade.

# JINGLE BELLS!

The name Santa Claus really comes from 'Saint Nicholas'. Nicholas lived on the Greek island of Myra, 800 years ago. He was a kind bishop, who gave money to a poor family and, it is said, helped sailors by calming stormy seas.

Nicholas became famous for his good deeds. After he died, the Church made him into a saint. The feast day of Saint Nicholas was first celebrated only on 6th December. But this secret giver of presents later became part of Christmas goodness - and excitement!

People from Holland took the idea to the United States and made the character we know today. At first, he was dressed in green - the green of kind winter spirits from ages past. But over 100 years ago in America, a cartoonist called Nast drew him with a bright red robe. Santa Claus had arrived!

In Finland, Father Christmas loads his reindeer sleigh.

19

# A Merry Christmas!

Father Christmas arrives in a surfers' rescue boat in Sydney, Australia.

CHRISTMAS DAY in a sleepy snow-clad village, or on a hot sandy beach. How do people all over the world celebrate? And what happens in Bethlehem, the very birthplace of Jesus Christ?

Excited fingers open presents pulled out from a Christmas stocking.

## THE WORLD AT CHRISTMAS

It's 25th December - Christmas Day for most Christians throughout the world. Some have already celebrated Christmas the night before. So today is a time for rest and for thinking what Christmas really means to them.

For others, whether in frosty air or hot sunlight, there is great excitement. Families and friends gather. Presents are opened. The church, shining with

lights, opens its doors. In cold climates, a feast is laid out on the table. In hot lands, it is spread out on a picnic cloth!

But what of Bethlehem, where it all started so long ago? The birthplace of Jesus is marked on the floor of a lamp-lit cave with a silver star. Over that cave is a church - the Church of the Nativity. At Christmas time, Christians flock here to see where their faith began.

It is believed that this star marks the spot where Jesus Christ was born. It is set in the floor of a cave in Bethlehem.

Outside is an open space called Nativity Square. Hymns and Christmas greetings are blared out for the crowds. There are lights and gift shops, the same as anywhere else.

# Christmas dinner

A T CHRISTMAS, people in different parts of the world have always eaten their special treats, from roast turkey to boiled turtle. They finish off with colourful cakes and fruity puddings and pies.

A Russian family enjoying a traditional Christmas dinner. Cheers!

## MEAT TREATS

Tastes for Christmas meat dishes have changed over time. Turkey is now a great favourite in many parts of the world. But chicken is still the festive dish in Africa and regions of South America. A hundred years ago, goose was the dish of the day. Early settlers in Canada enjoyed nothing better than a piece of boiled buffalo. And on an Australasian island, turtle was the thing to eat.

Even further back in time, rich people ate all sorts of exotic birds at Christmas - from guinea fowl to peacock.

Many of us also eat pork sausages and ham. Eating pork goes back to a time when pigs and wild boar were sacrificed to please the god of the sun. Pig-killings and boar hunts still go on at this time in parts of Europe. In the far north of Europe, people make special Christmas biscuits - in the shape of a pig!

## PUDDINGS, PIES AND ALL THINGS NICE

In Germany, Christmas food fairs are held in many of the cities. Brightly-lit stalls are piled high with spiced cakes and coloured marzipans. In Spain and Italy, all kinds of nutty nougats are

Many people eat roast turkey at Christmas.

Sweets and cakes of all types are sold at this Christmas market in Nuremberg in Germany.

a Christmas treat. Nougat was brought to southern Europe by people of a very different faith - the Muslim Moors from North Africa.

The Portuguese make huge round cakes with a hole in the centre. They are decorated with plump, juicy glacé fruits - oranges and limes, cherries and plums. In England, heavy steamed puddings and little round pies are full of dried fruit. But long ago, they were made with meat!

## ON THE FEAST OF STEPHEN

It's the day after Christmas. Now everyone can relax. But it is also the Feast of Saint Stephen, the first Christian to die for his faith. For parts of Europe it is also a time for hunting and horse-riding. In England, it is 'Boxing Day'. During Victorian times, servants were given boxes of gifts on the day after Christmas.

23

# And a Happy New Year!

WHAT COULD BE MORE EXCITING than Christmas? For many people, New Year on 1st January is the most important winter festival. Long ago, darkness and evil were finally swept away at this time.

## WHAT'S YOUR RESOLUTION?

Eight hundred years ago, many people celebrated Christmas at New Year. The birth of Christ and the birth of a hopeful new year were brought together. Many of the old New Year customs have now been moved to Christmas Day – but making a resolution is a New Year tradition.

A New Year's resolution is a promise to do something good or to behave better for the whole year! This is the birth of something new in our own lives. But how long can you keep your resolution? It isn't easy.

In Paris, France, Christmas lights shine on into New Year.

## DANCING IN THE STREETS

There are so many ways to celebrate New Year. On New Year's Eve in most of the world's capital cities, young people fill the squares. Sometimes they dance under freezing cold fountains! But there are older customs that still live on. In Philadelphia in the United States, mummers in amazing costumes play banjos as they parade through the streets. These actors mime scenes and folk stories from long ago. They clown around, too!

Mummers dance through the streets in Philadelphia, USA, to the sound of banjos.

## KNOCKING ON THE DOOR AT MIDNIGHT

In Scotland, New Year's Eve is known as Hogmanay, which probably means 'gift'. Giving is part of the fun of the first-footing ceremony, which takes place at the chimes of midnight on New Year's Eve. The first person to pass through the front door as the new year is rung in is given a special welcome. The first-footer knocks on the door and carries in gifts of food – or coal!

Scottish bagpipes are played at Hogmanay.

25

# The coming of the kings

CHRISTMAS ENDS ON THE TWELFTH DAY - the 6th January - with Epiphany. This reminds Christians how God showed Himself to the world through Jesus Christ. It also marks the arrival of the three kings to Bethlehem.

This picture of the three kings was painted over 600 years ago.

## GREAT KINGS BOW DOWN

This is the last part of our story. It tells of the journey of three kings to Bethlehem. They came from far-off lands - perhaps from the East and Africa. All of them knew from their studies that a great king, Jesus Christ, had just been born. So they set out to greet Him, guided by the bright star that shone over the stable. But their journey was not a smooth one.

Do you remember mean King Herod from the first part of the Christmas story? Well, the kings stopped by at his palace and told him of the new-born king. Herod was jealous and deeply alarmed. So he told the kings that when they found the baby, they should come back and tell him. Herod said that he wanted to greet the baby, but really he wanted to kill him!

The kings promised to return and went on their way to Bethelehem. There they knelt at Christ's feet and offered gifts of gold, sweet-smelling incense and myrrh. Before they left, they were told in a dream to steer clear of Herod. So the three kings returned home a different way - and the newborn baby was safe.

# ON THE TWELFTH DAY OF CHRISTMAS

So it's the Twelfth Day of Christmas - things are coming to an end. In many homes, this is when the last chocolate on the tree is eaten and the decorations all come down. But in some parts of the world, the celebrations have only just begun! In parts of South America, people in bright costumes dance and parade in the streets. In Mexico, a rich Twelfth-Day cake is baked.

In Spain, it is believed that the three kings pass by every house to leave gifts. And the children leave out their shoes. They are filled with straw for those hungry camels that carried the three kings all the way to Bethlehem.

In Bethlehem, the Greek Orthodox Church holds its Christmas celebrations. They take place on the 6th January.

Young kings ride to the Festival of the Kings in Ecuador on 6th January. This is Christmas time for people there.

# Let's celebrate!

You too can join in the celebrations. Try making this pop-up card and some Christmas crackers. You can get lots of ideas for decorating them by looking at the pictures in the book.

## MAKING A CHRISTMAS CARD

You will need:

1  card
2  paints, felt-tip pens or crayons
3  safe scissors
4  PVA glue
5  decorations such as glitter, sequins and ribbons

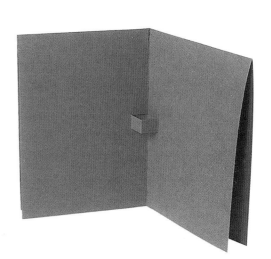

All you need to do is:

1  Fold the card in half one way – then fold it the other way. Look at the picture to help you.

2  Cut two slits on the inside of the card as shown in the picture. Then lift the strip of card so that it sticks out in a 'seat shape'.

3  Draw a picture on the front of the card. Or cut one out from wrapping paper or old Christmas cards. Then stick them to the card. Use lots of colourful decoration.

4  To make the inside 'pop-up': Make another picture on a separate piece of card. Try to keep it a simple shape such as a holly leaf or a snowman. Stick it onto the front part of the lifted 'seat' shape strip of card.

Now your card will fold flat – and a picture will pop up when you open it!

# MAKING CHRISTMAS CRACKERS

You will need:

1 crêpe paper and drawing paper
2 an empty kitchen roll cut into three to make three crackers
3 cracker fillers such as sweets, pencil sharpeners, erasers or balloons
4 paints, felt-tip pens or crayons
5 PVA glue
6 decorations such as sequins and glitter

All you need to do is:

1 Cut out the crêpe paper and drawing paper as shown in the picture. You could paint a picture or write a joke on the drawing paper.
2 Place the cracker filler inside the kitchen roll.
3 Roll the drawing paper round the kitchen roll. Stick the paper down lightly.
4 Roll all this in the crêpe paper. Stick the crêpe paper down. Now tuck the crêpe paper into the holes of the drawing paper and kitchen roll. Leave some at the ends for pulling!
5 You can now decorate your cracker brightly.

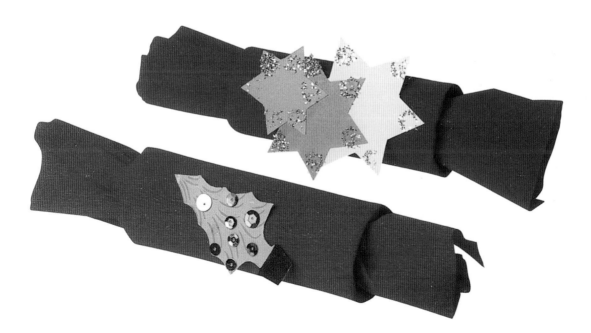

# Glossary

**angel**  a messenger of God
**bishop**  a senior priest in the Christian Church
**celebrate**  to show that a certain day or event is special
**ceremonies**  more solemn ways of celebrating a special day
**fast**  to eat only certain foods, or nothing at all – often as part of a religious custom
**hymn**  a religious song
**manger**  an eating trough for animals such as oxen and asses
**mummers**  actors in folk-plays
**pantomine**  a lively, colourful play, held mostly at Christmas
**saint**  a good person, thought to be especially holy after they have died
**spirits**  beings that you can't see – a bit like ghosts
**tradition**  a custom – a way of doing something passed down from parents

# Index